Can(am)asta™

# Can(am)asta™
## The Official Handbook

Hinda Packard
and Nancy Kaplan

iUniverse

# CAN(AM)ASTA™
## THE OFFICIAL HANDBOOK

*iUniverse books may be ordered through booksellers or by contacting:*

*iUniverse*
*1663 Liberty Drive*
*Bloomington, IN 47403*
*www.iuniverse.com*
*1-800-Authors (1-800-288-4677)*

*Because of the dynamic nature of the Internet, any web addresses or links contained in this book may have changed since publication and may no longer be valid. The views expressed in this work are solely those of the author and do not necessarily reflect the views of the publisher, and the publisher hereby disclaims any responsibility for them.*

*Any people depicted in stock imagery provided by Getty Images are models, and such images are being used for illustrative purposes only. Certain stock imagery © Getty Images.*

*ISBN: 978-1-5320-4869-2 (sc)*
*ISBN: 978-1-5320-4870-8 (e)*

*Print information available on the last page.*

*iUniverse rev. date: 12/27/2018*

# Acknowledgments

Our special thanks to our husbands, who have been extremely tolerant of our time away for the preparation of this book and, of course, our time away playing this wonderful game.

Just for your interest, our husbands have also learned the game from us, and as a result of playing, they have cemented a wonderful friendship between them.

We would like to thank the countless number of people who began as our eager students and became skilled and talented players. As with every learning experience, the inspiration goes both ways. As a result, we have built strong mutual friendships along the way. We would also like to thank Patti Greenberg for her photography expertise as well as Marlene Reich and Isobel Salmanovich for their valued input in the preparation of this handbook.

After reading this book, should you have any questions, please feel free to contact us at <u>canastajustforfun7@bell.ca</u>. Watch for our exciting new webpage, coming soon to Facebook, "CCL : (Canadian Can[Am] asta™ League).

# About the Authors

Hinda was born and raised in Montreal. She attended McGill University and later founded the Diabetic Association of Ville St. Laurent in Quebec, Canada. During that time, she coauthored, at the request of Health Canada, a multiethnic cookbook entitled *Taste-Tingling Ethnic Dishes: Recipes from Ten Ethnic Groups.* She has two married daughters and four beautiful grandchildren. When she is not teaching or playing canasta, she is playing with her grandchildren. She is retired and discovered the love of canasta over the past many years. She is married and currently living in a suburb of Montreal.

Nancy was born in New Brunswick. She grew up in Cape Breton, Nova Scotia. A graduate of Dalhousie University, work brought her to Montreal, where she began her profession as an educator and dental hygienist in the public system. Her expertise in teaching throughout her forty-five-year professional span has contributed to the writing of this handbook. She is happily married and has one daughter and three stepsons. She is the grandmother of seven grandchildren.

# Contents

# Introduction

When my friend Hinda Packard asked me to collaborate on writing a book on canasta, we thought, What a perfect partnership for us! Our friendship is just like a Can(Am)asta™ game—a partnership where if we follow the rules, we can win. Can(Am)asta™ is like this friendship. One has to communicate clearly to get what one wants. One has to listen well, follow rules, and develop strategies. In the game of life and friendship, those rules are cardinal.

We love canasta, yet as we were learning to play, it became obvious to us that every person we spoke to had a different set of rules, some very easy and some very challenging. For this handbook, we accumulated an endless number of handouts from many sources, both Canadian and American canasta groups of players, and then extrapolated and perfected the information to formulate this handbook. Through this combination of rules, we hope you will find the game of Can(Am) asta™ fun and, at the same time, competitive and stimulating.

Today is the start of a Can(Am)asta™ day with your friends. The cards have been shuffled and dealt, and now the fun begins.

This handbook combines the American canasta teachings with more challenging modifications to make the game more thought-provoking and intriguing. In this handbook, you will learn the basics. Once you have mastered them, this handbook will teach you strategies to make your game more interesting. Of course, luck plays a part, as in any other game, but with the addition of jokers and wild cards, the game is more viable and accepting.

If you have ever played canasta or taken any structured canasta courses, this book will help you learn and cement the strategies of the game. During most of these courses, there is not enough available time to teach a systematic plan of action. As you learn more strategies, you will be adding depth and perception to your game.

When you begin to play Can(Am)asta™, many questions will arise as to how to strategically play your hand. In this handbook, you will learn how to sharpen your learned skills and then subsequently hone the strategies of the game. It will help you gain confidence with your choices.

We have written this handbook in a deliberate fashion. For those of you who are detailed learners, you may find the rules and definitions a little repetitive. For those of you who just want to play the game or find specific rulings or strategies, this format is for you. And for those who are searching for Canadian and American rules, this handbook is your guide. You can use this handbook to learn the basics. With every game you play, your strategies for winning will become more apparent. Armed with the knowledge gained from this handbook, you will be able to join a game with other players from all over the world. Our advice is to always ask, "What are your table rules?" before playing the game.

By reading this handbook, you will be passing many happy hours of Can(Am)asta™, using your brain, meeting some challenges, being a partner, and possibly developing new lifelong friendships. That is what happened to us, and, yes, this game of Can(Am)asta™ may just exercise your brain cells to be more active, entertained, and alive for many more years to come.

May this new obsession replace other not-so-healthy inclinations. We promise you that playing Can(Am)asta™ will bring you much joy and comfort.

Enjoy and please embrace this book.

Hinda Packard and Nancy Kaplan

# Two-Deck Canasta—History

ca·nas·ta (kə-năs'tə) n.

1.  A card game for two to six players, requiring two or three decks of cards, in which the object is to obtain melds of three or more cards of the same rank.

2.  A meld of seven cards having the same rank in this game.

[Spanish canasta, *basket, canasta (in reference to the container or tray used to hold the piles of undrawn and discarded cards when playing the game)*, from canasto, *basket with a narrowing opening* (influenced by cesta, *basket*), from Latin canistrum; see canister.]

The game of canasta was devised by Segundo Santos and Alberto Serrato in Montevideo, Uruguay, in 1939.[1] In the 1940s, the game quickly spread in myriad variations to Chile, Peru, Brazil, and Argentina,[2] where its rules were further refined[3] before being introduced to the United States in 1948, where it was then referred to as the Argentine rummy game by Ottilie H. Reilly in 1949 and Michael Scully of *Coronet* magazine in 1953.[4] The game quickly became a card-craze boom in the 1950s,[5] providing a sales avalanche of card sets, card trays, and books about the subject.[6]

In this version, players use two decks, including the four jokers (totaling 108 cards), a card tray, and a score sheet.

---

[1]   *American Heritage Dictionary of the English Language*, 5th Edition (Houghton Mifflin Harcourt Publishing Company, 2016).

[2]   *American Heritage Dictionary Spanish Word Histories and Mysteries: English Words that Come from Spanish* (Houghton Mifflin Harcourt, 2007).

[3]   John Scarne, *Scarne on Card Games* (Dover Publications, 2004), 127.

[4]   John Griswold, *Ian Fleming's James Bond: Annotations and Chronologies for Ian Fleming's Bond Stories* (Bloomington: AuthorHouse, 2006), 228.

[5]   Nikki Katz, *The Everything Card Games Book* (Adams Media, 2004), 52.

[6]   *Life*, December 19, 1949.

## Definitions

### BASE SCORE

This includes the total points for all your threes (3s), your completed canastas, the 100 points for cutting the deck exactly, and the 100 points for going out. Points are either positive or negative, depending on the number of completed canastas. With no canastas, your points are all negative. With one canasta, the threes (3s) are not counted; they are neutral. With two or more canastas, all points are positive.

### BLACK, DIRTY, UNNATURAL CANASTA

These terms all mean the same. This contains up to two wild cards in the seven-card canasta and is equal to 300 points.

# CANASTA

Canasta refers to seven like cards (e.g., all sixes, eights, nines, tens, jokers, queens, or kings) or five to six like cards (with wild cards completing the seven-card requirement).

# CARD POINT COUNT

| Cards | Points |
|-------|--------|
| 4–7 | 5 points |
| 8–kings | 10 points |
| aces | 20 points |
| deuces (2s) | 20 points |
| jokers | 50 points |

# CLEAN, RED, PURE, OR NATURAL CANASTA

These terms all mean the same. They refer to a set of natural cards that do not include any wild cards and are equal to 500 points.

# CLEAN TRIPLE

This refers to three cards of the same rank (e.g., 6, 6, 6 or king, king, king) without any wild cards.

# THE CUT OR DEAL

These words mean the same. The cards are cut. The top cards are used to make the talons and the last eight cards of the pack. The bottom cards are used to deal four sets of thirteen cards each (fifty-two cards total). Cards are dealt clockwise. Each player receives thirteen cards.

# DEAD CARD

This is a card that matches a completed canasta. This is considered a safe card to throw. However, this card can never be thrown onto an empty tray.

# THE DECK

The deck consists of 108 cards, comprising two fifty-two-card decks plus four jokers. These two decks are then shuffled together.

# DIRTY PACK

A pack is deemed dirty if there are either three or more sevens or three or more aces discarded in the pack.

# DISCARD

This is the card thrown onto the pack, faceup, once a turn has ended. This card can never be a wild card.

# FIFTH OR SIXTH POSITION

This term refers to any meld or column that has five or six cards (of the seven required cards) needed to complete a canasta.

# GAME

A game consists of several plays and ends when one team achieves a total score of 8,500 points.

# HAND

A hand consists of cards held by the player. A hand also denotes one of the special hands—for example, a pairs hand or a garbage hand.

# INITIAL MELD

This applies to when one of the partners opens, and this is considered the first turn during a hand when the player puts down one or more melds or columns to open. When doing this, you must meet the minimum point-count requirement, in terms of the total value of cards that you put down. Therefore, after you or your partner have successfully made your initial meld or column(s), both of you can freely put down cards throughout the round, bringing you closer to the 8,500 point goal.

# MELDS OR COLUMN

These terms mean the same. A meld or column can never contain more than seven cards. A meld or column is constructed by laying a set of three to seven matching cards from a player's hand onto the table faceup. Wild cards may be used as substitutes for one or two of the natural cards, but the meld or column must always include a minimum of two natural cards initially, for example, two kings and one or two wild cards.

# MELD SCORE

This includes the total points for all your completed canastas as well as for your incomplete melds or columns on the table. Points are either positive or negative, depending on whether you have completed at least one canasta during the round of play. If you have not been able to make a canasta, then all these totals are counted against you and are in the negative.

# TO OPEN

To open (i.e., to start making canastas), one needs the following:

| 125 points | for | 0–2,999 total score points |
|---|---|---|
| 155 points | for | 3,000–4,999 total score points |
| 180 points | for | 5,000–8,500 total score points |

# OPENING OR INITIAL

An opening meld (also called an initial meld) consists of one or more columns that meet the opening point criteria. Only one member of the team is permitted to open. The other team (opponents) still must open. This opening meld must include a minimum of three or more identical cards, which is called a clean triple, plus any number of mixed melds (which can contain wild cards). All these cards must meet the opening point requirement for that particular round.

# PACK

The pack refers to the cards that have been discarded.

# PLAY OR ROUND

These terms mean the same. A play or round begins with the distribution of cards and ends when one player discards his or her last card. The opponent to the dealer's left begins first. The play or round moves clockwise. The individual play or round consists of a player making a draw by either picking a card from the stockpile or by picking the pack.

## PURE ACE CANASTA

A pure ace canasta has the following rules: no wild cards allowed; 2,500 points if completed; minus 2,500 points if not completed on the table; and minus 1,500 points if you have three or more aces remaining in your hand at end of the game.

Note—never put jokers or deuces (2s) with aces except to open. During the game, aces may be melded at any time but must be pure, clean, or natural (i.e., with no wild cards).

## SAFE CARD

This card is one that is identical to your opponent's already completed canasta or is one that is identical to your opponent's meld or column that is in the fifth or sixth position on the table.

## SEVENS

Completed, it is worth 2,500 points; if incomplete, it is minus 2,500 points when on the table and minus 1,500 points when you have three or more sevens remaining in your hand at the end of the game.

## STOCKPILE

The stockpile is the deck of closed cards from which all players draw at each turn. It can also be called the source deck.

## STRANGE OR FOREIGN CARD

These terms mean the same—a card that is not the same as your incomplete canastas or melds and is not identical to your completed canastas. This is the last card thrown down in order for you to go out.

# TALON OR BONUS PACK

Both mean the same. While the dealer is dealing, the cutter makes four piles from the bottom of the deck: three piles of four cards and one pile of three cards. The cutter then makes three separate stacks: one stack of eight cards, by combining the first pile of four cards and the other pile of four cards; one stack of four cards; and one stack of three cards. The stacks of three cards and four cards are placed around the card tray, and the stack of eight cards is placed sideways. Then the remaining cards are to be placed on top of these eight cards.

a) The first team to meld or open picks up the four-card talon after discarding their card, thus ending their turn.

b) The second team to meld or open then picks up the three-card talon after discarding their card, thus ending their turn.

c) A player may not be reminded to pick up their talon and may not pick up the talon until he or she discards a card.

d) If a talon is not picked up before the player to the left draws his or her next card or picks the pack, the talon is forfeited. You snooze … you lose!

# THREES (3S)

Threes are special cards. They are kept separately as to color (red and black) and are counted by color. Threes (3s) are not kept in your hand and are not used for canastas, except for doing a special dream hand. They are placed facedown on the table. At your turn, you expose these threes (3s) and replace each of them with another card from the stockpile. As you play, you always replace threes (3s) with another card. However, if you receive a three (3) in one of the two bonus packs (talon—received once you open), you do not take an additional card to replace the three (3).

Remember the threes (3s) are only bonus points that you accumulate after completing two canastas:

One (1) three = 100 points
Two (2) threes = 300 points
Three (3) threes = 500 points
Four (4) threes = 1,000 points
For example:
1 red three and 1 black three = 100 + 100 = 200 points
2 red threes = 300 points

When counting points for threes (3s), think 1, 2, 3, 4 = 100, 300, 500, 1,000.

Note—if you only have one canasta, the threes (3s) are not counted as part of your score. Two or more canastas make the bonus values in the plus—that is, the threes (3s) are bonus points to count as 100, 300, 500, and 1,000.

## TOTAL SCORE

The total score is the total of both the base score and the meld score.

## TURN

Each player begins his or her turn by either drawing a card from the stockpile (also called the source deck) or by picking up the discarded deck (called the pack) and ends his or her turn by either discarding a card to the discarded deck or pack or by melding one of the special hands.

## WILD CARDS

The deuces (2s) and jokers are considered wild cards. Deuces (2s) are worth 20 points, and jokers are worth 50 points. During the game, wild cards can be used as substitutes (with some restrictions) for a natural card of any rank (e.g., joker-joker-joker-2 or 6-6-6-6-6-2-joker). There are restrictions as to when you may use these jokers and deuces, depending on the type of canasta game being played.

## WILD CARD CANASTA

It is possible to put down an initial meld or column of only wild cards. This is possible when the points add up to the minimum requirement needed to open. In this case, you do not then need a clean or pure meld or column in addition to this.

1. Upon completion of this canasta, jokers and deuces (2s) equal 2,500 points and all deuces (2s) are 3,000 points.

# Objectives

The objective of the game of Can(Am)asta™ is to score points by melding cards and completing canastas. The game of Can(Am)asta™ requires two decks of cards including the four jokers for a total of 108 cards (which includes eight deuces). A canasta consists of either seven like cards or five to six like cards with one or two wild cards. A round ends when the stockpile is depleted or when a team makes two or more canastas and either partner on that team is able to properly dispose of all cards and still has a strange discard to end the game. This is called going out, and the team gets an additional 100 points. The melds or columns you or your partner make belong to your team. You need a score pad, a pencil or pen, and a canasta tray.

- ☐ Remember: no more than two wild cards are allowed in each canasta.
- ☐ Thirteen cards are dealt to each of the four players.
- ☐ To win a canasta game, you must acquire 8,500 points or more first.

☐ A canasta is seven cards of the same number (e.g., 5, 5, 5, 5, 5, 5, 5).

☐ A pure, clean, or natural canasta is seven of a kind (e.g., 5, 5, 5, 5, 5, 5, 5) and is worth 500 points. A red card is then put on top. All these terms mean the same.

☐ A mixed, unnatural, or dirty canasta is when one or two deuces or jokers are used as a wild card(s) to make a canasta. This is worth 300 points. A black card is then put on top. All these terms mean the same.

☐ To open, you need the following:

| 125 points | for | 0–2,999 total score points |
|---|---|---|
| 155 points | for | 3,000–4,999 total score points |
| 180 points | for | 5,000–8,500 total score points |

☐ To open for your initial meld:

1) When melding initially, you must include at least one clean (natural or pure) triple (or more) in addition to other cards to make the point count. The exception is when melding wild cards only.

2) If you start to open or meld and do not have the right count, you are then penalized 10 additional points (e.g., if you need 125 points to open, you now need 135 points to open on your next attempt).

☐ Threes (3s) are special cards. They are kept separately as to color (red and black) and are counted by color. Threes (3s) are not kept in your hand and are not used for canastas, except for a special hand. They are placed on the table as soon as you get one and are replaced with another card that you pick up from the pack. If you receive any threes (3s) in one of the two bonus packs or talons (received once you open), you do not take an additional card to replace this three (3).

☐ You must have at least two canastas to go out.

# How to Play the Game (Four Players)

1. There are four players in specific partnerships.
2. The partners sit opposite each other. The shuffled pack is cut; then the top section of the deck is used for the talon distribution. The remaining pack is used to deal four thirteen-card hands. In the center of the table, there is a facedown pile of cards called the stockpile and a space for the faceup pile of cards called the discard pile (pack).
3. One person shuffles and then cuts the two decks. The shuffled pack is cut, and then the top section of the deck is used for the talon distribution (using fifteen cards) and is dealt from the bottom of that distribution. The remaining pack is used to deal the four thirteen-card hands (total fifty-two cards). Tip—remember T (top), T (talon), B (bottom), D(deal) = T–T; B–D.

4. The cutter then collects the first pile of four and the third pile of four, combines them, and then places them across the tray under the stockpile of unexposed cards, thus showing that the end of the game is near.

5. The four- and three-card pile are placed on opposite sides of the tray facedown. These piles are called your talons and are picked up during the game if deemed necessary. If a three (3) is in one of these two piles, you do not replace it with another card upon your turn. It will be counted in your total threes (3s) at the end of your round.

6. The game (play) always goes clockwise (i.e., the first person to play is left of the dealer).

7. The players across from each other are partners.

8. The object is to get as many points as possible.

9. To win the game, one of the two teams must reach 8,500 points.

10. **How to Play The player to the left of the dealer goes first. A basic turn consists of picking the top card of the stockpile and then adding it to your hand without showing anyone else that card. Your turn ends once you discard one card from your hand faceup on top of the pack. Instead of picking a card from the stockpile, you may pick the pack, providing you meet the requirements of this privilege. Place like cards together. To begin the game, place threes (3s) facedown on the table, and when it is your turn, face them up as you replace those cards. (Threes [3s] are never used for melding, except for a special hand.) Each player, in turn, continues in this manner until one of the partners has enough points to open, placing the initial melds or columns open in front of them.**

11. The play ends when a player goes out (i.e., disposes of all the cards in his or her hand, ending with a strange card and completing a minimum of two canastas).

12. Completed canastas can have up to two wild cards.

13. Always count and make sure the point value of the cards you are putting down is correct to open before exposing them to the other players. Remember—if your point count is incorrect, then you and

your partner will be penalized 10 additional points on your next attempt to open.

14. The first person to open gets the four-card pile or talon. Pick up the talon immediately after melding, or you will lose it. Your partner is not allowed to remind you to pick up the talon. A strategy to help remember to pick up the bonus talon, after opening or melding is for the other partner to say, "Thank you, partner," after his or her partner discards the card ending his or her turn. This is an unconventional way to remind yourself or your partner about the talon without any actual table talk directives.

15. The three-card pile or talon then goes to the next person who opens on the opposite team. If neither team opens, then the three- and four-card piles or talons remain untouched.

To meld (to put down on the table), you must have a minimum of at least three like cards (a triple) or more and two like cards with a wild card, and what you put down must equal the minimum required points to open.

16. During the game, whoever takes the ninth-to-last card must announce to everyone that there are now eight cards left.

17. To go out, you must have at least two canastas. There is no difference if they are natural or mixed, and you must end with a strange or foreign card.

18. If you have only one canasta at the end of the game, then your threes (3s) are not counted for any points—they are neutral.

19. If you have no canastas at the end of the game, then all your points are counted as minus (including the value points of the threes [3s]).

20. You must ask your partner if you can go out before actually going out. You can only ask your partner once during a round of play.

21. If you pick up the pack to open or meld, you must have three face cards of that top card on the pack. You must empty the pack when you pick it up (i.e., any card that matches what is already down (even one card) or anything that you have three or more of in the pack (even sevens [7s] and aces) must be put down.

22. If you pick up the pack during the game, once you have opened, you must have two face cards of that top card on the pack. You must empty the pack when you pick it up—that is, any card that matches what is already down (even one card) or anything that you have three or more of in the pack (even sevens [7s] and aces) must be put down.

23. Under some conditions, you may want to take the pack instead of picking from the stockpile. In order to do this, you must use the top card as part of your valid meld or column requirement. In this case, place the minimum required pair of cards from your hand faceup on the table, and then add the top card of the discard pile (pack) to them to achieve the necessary requirement. If you pick up the pack, you must put down the cards from your hand, facedown. You cannot combine these cards with the cards from the picked pack.

24. A natural canasta (all face-value cards) in your hand (and not picked from the discarded pack) is an automatic opening, even if it is not enough points to open. This is one of the garbage hands. It is worth 2,500 points, and the game continues. At other tables, this is worth 3,500 points, and the game stops. One of these two plays becomes a table rule for a natural canasta. This must be decided before starting the game.

25. If you open with a wild card meld or column, you must finish the wild card canasta before adding any other wild cards to other incomplete canastas. Wild cards can never be used with sevens (7s).

26. A wild card can be used on opening when combined with aces. However, the value of this completed canasta is only 300 points. If not completed, you are not penalized. This is the only time you can use wild cards with aces.

27. However, when opening or starting a clean or natural ace meld or column during the hand (i.e., without wild cards), if it is not completed, you are penalized 2,500 points.

28. During the game, you must put two cards down at a time from your hand. If, however, you are finishing a canasta that already has six cards in the meld or column (sixth position), you can put one card down for its completion.

29. When you have one wild card left in your hand and you pick up a three (3) from the stockpile, you must throw away the three (3) onto the pack (i.e., you must keep the wild card in your hand). However, should any of the other three players pick the pack, this three (3) cannot be used by anyone.

30. To go out, or finish the round, you must have at least two canastas. Then ask your partner first. You need a strange card to discard. You and your partner earn an extra 100 points for going out.

31. When the stockpile is completed, this normally ends the game. If, however, the person next in rotation has two or more face cards matching the last card thrown, he or she may pick the pack, if desired. That player then has to put down all relevant cards from the pack and discard a strange or foreign card, thus ending the game.

32. The game ends when one team reaches 8,500 points. If both teams have reached more than 8,500 points, then the higher score wins.

# Explanation of Play

## OPENING OR INITIAL MELD

The initial meld made by each team is subject to the following conditions:

1.  An opening meld consists of a minimum of a clean triple (or more) plus one or more additional melds or columns with wild cards. Additional melds or columns may consist of a pair with a wild card or clean triples.
2.  Two or more aces plus one or two wild cards may only be used as part of an opening meld.
3.  A natural canasta may be used for the opening meld. Note— this automatically satisfies the clean triple and point-count rules, no matter what the actual point count is. This is worth 2,500 or 3,500 points, depending on your table rules.
4.  A mixed canasta may be used as part of the opening meld, but the clean triple rule must still be satisfied.

5. A wild card canasta may be used for the opening meld as follows:
   - ☐ If the wild-card canasta meets the point-count requirement, it may be melded without the need of a clean triple.
   - ☐ But if you do not have the point count with the wild cards, your additional column must include a clean triple.
6. A pairs hand or any special hand may be used for the opening meld without regard to any of the preceding rules, and the round is over. The team that gets this special hand receives 3,500 points, and their opponents count their points as if the game ended normally.
7. If an opening meld is attempted but does not meet the point-count requirement, the point count is increased by 10 points for the player's next opening attempt.
8. An opening meld should be placed on the table in front of the player executing the meld, and any threes (3s) and closed canastas are managed by his or her partner.

## DISCARD

1. Once a card touches the table, it must be discarded (the player may not change his or her mind).
2. Threes may never be discarded onto the pack.
3. It is not permitted to discard a wild card. The exception is when the player is holding only wild cards in his or her hand. If the pack is picked up after a wild card has been discarded, this wild card cannot be used by anyone; it is a dead card.
4. Aces and sevens (7s) or any completed canastas may not be discarded to an empty discard tray.
5. Three face cards are required to pick up the pack upon opening, and this top card on the pack is included in your points needed to open, if necessary.
6. Once open, you only need two face cards to pick the pack.

7. Once a canasta is made, that number cannot be used again by you or your partner to start another canasta.

8. Once a canasta is made, you cannot look back at it, as it is very important to keep track of the number of wild cards used throughout the game as well as all sevens (7s) and aces.

9. The player who takes the turn cards announces, "Eight cards left."

## END OF THE PLAY OR GOING OUT

The round ends if a player goes out (must have two or more canastas) or if the stockpile becomes depleted so that a player who needs to draw a card cannot do so.

1. You can only go out if you can satisfy both of the following conditions:
   1) Your team has completed two canastas.
   2) You are able to put down all but one of your cards, and this last discard must be a strange card.

2. When you are in a position to go out, you must first ask your partner's permission. If you ask and your partner says yes, you must go out; if your partner says no, you cannot go out on that turn, and therefore, you must keep at least one card in your hand after discarding. If you have one canasta and one card in your hand and it is a wild card and you draw a wild card, you must throw the wild card. If you do intend to ask your partner for permission, you must first draw a card from the stockpile and then ask for permission. Then you must lay down your cards and go out (you cannot change your mind). You are not allowed to ask your partner a second time.

3. It often happens that the end of the stockpile is reached before anyone has gone out.

4. Threes (3s) cannot be discarded when going out. You must always have a strange card to throw out. You are allowed to

go out even if you have incomplete seven (7), ace, or wild card canastas on the table (i.e., 3s are never considered to be a strange card).

5.  At the end of the game, all players must display their hands for all others to see.

# CHAPTER

# Scoring

1. At the end of the round, each team adds up the remaining cards in their hand at face value.

2. The total sum of the cards remaining in both hands is removed from the melded cards on table and put back in the tray. (If you need to use a card or two from a closed canasta, take it from the bottom of the canasta, leaving the black or red card on top.)

3. Then add up the value of the threes (3s) (if any) and the value of all the closed canastas. That is part of your base score. Remember that if you only have one canasta, you do not get bonus credit for the threes (3s). They are neutral now.

4. Add up the value(s) of your completed canastas. Then add this score with the value of your threes (3s), thus equaling your base score total. Remember to add 100 additional points if your team has gone out.

5. After you have counted the threes (3s), put them aside. Add up all the cards on the table and the cards in the canastas at point

value. Make piles equaling 100 points for easy counting. This is your total meld score.

6. If you are lucky enough to acquire all eight threes (i.e., four red threes plus four black threes), then your team receives 100 additional points. This amount is added to your base score.

7. If you are lucky enough to have cut the deck exactly, so that there are exactly 52 cards to be dealt to each of the four players, then the team that cut the deck receives an additional 100 points. This amount is added to your base score.

8. If you are left with three or more wild cards in your hand, you are never penalized.

9. After your meld score is counted, put a three (3) on each pile. This will separate the threes (3s) in the deck when shuffling, leading to a better distribution of cards. Do the same distribution with jokers and deuces (2s) as needed.

10. If you do not make any canastas, you are minus all the threes (3s), all the cards on the table, and, of course, the cards left in your hand. Subtract this total from your previous total. If this is your first score, then you have a negative total.

11. At the end of the next round, repeat all the previous steps and do the scoring. Add it to your previous score.

12. When one team reaches 8,500 points or more, the game is over.

Scoring summarized …

| Scoring Item | Team has no complete canastas | Team has one complete canasta | Team has two or more complete canastas | Team goes out with a special hand |
|---|---|---|---|---|
| Bonus scores for canastas and for going out | does not apply | bonus added to score | bonus added to score | not counted |

| Scoring Item | Team has no complete canastas | Team has one complete canasta | Team has two or more complete canastas | Team goes out with a special hand |
|---|---|---|---|---|
| Penalties for incomplete canastas | penalty deducted from score | penalty deducted from score | penalty deducted from score | not counted |
| Bonuses or penalties for threes | penalty deducted from score | not counted | bonus added to score | not counted |
| Scores for melded cards | deducted from score | added to score | added to score | not counted |
| Penalties for cards remaining in players' hands | deducted from score | deducted from score | deducted from score | not counted |

## NOTE

If one team goes out with a special hand, the other team scores in the normal fashion (i.e., as if the game finished normally).

## PENALTIES FOR INCOMPLETE CANASTAS AND FOR INCOMPLETE ACES AND SEVENS

If a team has melded pure aces, sevens, or wild cards but has not completed a canasta of that type, then they are penalized as follows:

☐ for a pure ace meld or column of less than seven cards, minus 2,500 points

☐ for a sevens meld or column of less than seven cards, minus 2,500 points

☐ for a wild card meld or column of less than seven cards, minus 2,500 points

If a player has more than two aces or more than two sevens in their hand, then that player's team is penalized as follows:

☐ for three or more sevens remaining in a player's hand, minus 1,500 points

☐ for three or more aces remaining in a player's hand, minus 1,500 points

## SCORING

| | |
|---|---|
| 4, 5, 6, 7 | 5 points each |
| 8, 9, 10, jack, queen, king | 10 points each |
| Ace | 20 points each |
| deuce | 20 points each |
| joker | 50 points each |
| one red 3 (along with 2 or more canastas) | 100 points |
| two red 3s (along with 2 or more canastas) | 300 points |
| three red 3s (along with 2 or more canastas) | 500 points |
| four red 3s (along with 2 or more canastas) | 1,000 points |
| black 3s | same as for Red 3s |
| natural, clean, or pure canasta (no wild cards) | 500 points |
| unnatural or dirty canasta (with 1 or 2 wild cards) | 300 points |
| canasta of sevens (7s) | 2,500 points |
| canasta of all aces (no wild cards) | 2,500 points |
| canasta of jokers with 2s | 2,500 points |
| canasta of all 2s | 3,000 points |

| red canasta in hand during play (game continues) | 2,500 points |
| pairs hand | 3,500 points |
| garbage hand | 3,500 points |
| all other special hands (not included above) | 3,500 points |
| cutting the deck exactly so that there are fifty-two cards to be dealt to all four players | 100 points |
| going out | 100 points |
| having all eight 3s | 100 points |

## PENALTY SCORING

| incomplete 7s on table | minus 2,500 points |
| incomplete aces on table | minus 2,500 points |
| incomplete wild card canasta on table | minus 2,500 points |
| three or more aces in hand at end of game | minus 1,500 points |
| three or more 7s in hand at end of game | minus 1,500 points |
| incorrect attempt to open | 10 points added to next meld count upon opening |

CHAPTER

*Rules*

1. A canasta of sevens (7s) can never have a wild card. If completed, it is worth 2,500 points. If not completed, the team is penalized 2,500 points.
2. You can never throw a wild card onto the pack unless you have only wild cards in your hand. This hand then must be shown to everyone before you throw a wild card onto the pack. Should your partner or your opponents be able to pick the pack that contains this wild card, the wild card can never be used during this round.
3. You can never throw a three (3) onto the pack.
4. There should be no table talk during the game. This includes asking your partner where to place wild cards, how your hand looks, what your hand has or does not have, and so on. However, discussing a new piece of jewelry is acceptable!

5. When the dealer has exactly fifty-two cards to deal the four hands, then the cutter (and his or her partner) gets an additional 100 points at the end of the round.

6. When the game ends, if one or more players are holding three or more aces or sevens (7s) in their hands, those players' teams are penalized 1,500 points for each one. Should both partners have three or more sevens (7s) (or three or more aces) in their hands, then that team is penalized 1,500 points x 2 = 3,000 points! Should one partner have three or more aces in his or her hand and the other partner have three or more sevens (7s) in his or her hand, then the team is penalized 1,500 x 2 = 3,000 points.

7. A canasta using aces, only upon opening, may be made with or without wild cards. If started without a wild card, it must be completed without a wild card, and if completed, it is worth 2,500 points. If not completed, the team is penalized 2,500 points. If an ace canasta is started by picking a discarded ace from the pack (either upon opening or during the round), it must be completed without wild cards (pure or clean).

8. The only time an ace canasta may have wild cards is when the team uses them in the opening meld. Then it is considered as if it were a black canasta and is worth 300 points if made. There is no penalty if not made.

9. If you and your partner have completed an ace canasta and then one of you pick the pack and there are three or more aces in the pack, you do not have to put these aces on the table, because you have already completed an ace canasta and you can never have two identical canastas. You are also not penalized if you are holding three aces in your hand after picking the pack, should your opponents go out immediately after you have picked the pack. However, you must throw an ace on your next turn so that you will not be caught with three or more aces, as your saving grace period has ended.

10. To open (i.e., to start making canastas), you need the following.

| 125 points | for | 0–2,999 total score points |
| 155 points | for | 3,000–4,999 total score points |
| 180 points | for | 5,000–8,500 total score point |

11. Upon opening, a clean, pure, or natural column consists of a minimum of three cards of the same rank. On your partner's next turn, you may then add cards of the same rank, and these cards may contain wild cards, unless your team began a column of wild cards. Remember: if you start a column of wild cards, this column must be finished first before you can add a wild card to any additional column, and conversely, once opened and there are wild cards already down on the table, you cannot start a wild card canasta until those melds or columns containing the wild cards have been completed.

12. Pick up the talon immediately after melding, or you will lose it. If you snooze, you lose!

13. Once you or your partner have opened (made your meld[s]), either you or your partner can pick up the pack on the tray if you have two of the same cards that are being discarded by your opponent.

14. If you and your partner have opened and you have a meld or column in the fifth or sixth position (i.e., there are five or six cards in that column), you cannot pick the pack should you be holding two like cards of the same discarded card to complete your canasta. Rationale—if you already have two face cards in your hand, thus enabling you to complete the canasta from your hand, then you do not need that third card from the pack.

15. If a team makes no canastas, all points are deducted from their score, including your threes (3s).

16. If a team makes only one canasta, the total value of the threes (3s) is not deducted and also not credited; they are neutral.

17. If a team makes two or more canastas, the total value of the threes (3s) accumulated is credited (this is called "making the threes good")—100, 300, 500, or 1,000.

18. Once a canasta is made, that card cannot be used in another meld or column canasta, even with a wild card by the same team—that is, cannot have two identical canastas. This does not affect your opponents.

19. When there is only one card on the pack and you wish to pick up this card, you cannot because there would not be another card from the pack to discard. You must always have one card to discard from the pack you picked. Therefore, the first card thrown onto an empty tray is considered a frozen card.

20. Players must announce when they have three or fewer cards left in their hand.

21. Each time a false initial meld is made, the required points for melding is increased by 10 points.

22. If a team fails to complete one canasta, the value of all cards held by both players, plus the cards melded and accumulated threes (3s), are deducted from the team's score.

23. On an empty tray, you can never discard an ace, a seven (7), or any closed, completed, or finished canastas (i.e., if you have completed a canasta of fours, then you cannot discard a four onto an empty tray).

24. When you want to start a wild card canasta during the round and there is a meld or column that already has one or two wild cards, then you cannot start this wild card canasta until that particular meld or column has been completed. Once you have started a wild card canasta, there cannot be any wild cards in any other meld or column on the table.

25. You are never allowed to have more than one meld or column of the same rank. However, it is possible for both teams to start a meld or column of the same rank, but obviously, one team will never be able to complete that meld or column.

26. You and your partner must have at least two canastas to go out.

27. Upon completion of any of the special hands (i.e., pair; garbage; splash; 3, 3, 4, 4; two canastas in hand; and dream hands) (using a total of fourteen cards) the game stops. Your partner's hand does not count, even if he or she is holding more than three sevens (7s) or more than three aces. The threes (3s) are not counted as well (they are ignored). The opponents' hands are counted as if the game had ended normally.

28. When the last card is thrown on the tray, the next player (opponent) may pick the pack, if he or she has two face cards matching the last card thrown. The opponent then discards all cards from the pack and throws a card from the pack signaling the end of the game.

8

♥

CHAPTER

## Strategies

1. Try to pick the pack often. You will accumulate more points. Canastas demand a lot of cards, and the best way to acquire cards is by repeatedly picking the pack.

2. It is a very helpful strategy to pick the pack often. However, this also prolongs the game. If you feel that prolonging the round may be useful to your opponents, then try to end the game quickly, providing you have a minimum of two canastas completed. However, if you feel that prolonging the round may be useful to you and your partner, then by all means continue picking the pack as often as you can.

3. Try to avoid giving the pack to opponents by throwing new cards.

4. A safe card to throw to your opponents is a card matching one of their melds or columns that is in the fifth position or sixth position (i.e., any one of their melds or columns that has five or six cards already down), as they cannot pick the pack with this

card. It is also totally safe to throw down a card that is identical to the one that has been used for their completed canasta (i.e., if they have completed a canasta of eights [8s], then it is safe to throw an eight [8]), as they cannot start another canasta of the same number.

5. When trying to open, hold higher point cards and discard lower point cards.

6. Watch cards that are being thrown, especially by the opponent you are throwing to. (If they throw a king, it might be safe for you to throw a king, so they won't pick the pack.) Also watch what your partner throws as well.

7. Throw from a triple. Sometimes instead of putting down a meld or column of three cards (e.g., 6, 6, 6,) you might want to discard one of the sixes (6s), keeping two in your hand so that the opponent who throws to you will think it is a safe card to throw. Then you can pick the pack.

8. If you have two canastas and opponents have not gone down or made a canasta yet, try to go out early, so opponents will get caught with their card points and their threes (3s).

9. Always try to keep count of all discarded cards.

10. Try to develop your memory by concentrating on your left opponent's discards, followed by the cards that have been discarded in the pack, and third by your partner's and your right opponent's discards.

11. At any time, but especially if you need 180 points to open and you have few or no wild cards and few points, try going for a special hand. Then you don't need to count points, and the game ends.

12. Always silently count the number of aces and sevens (7s) discarded in the pack. You don't want to get caught with more than two of each at the end of a round.

13. Signaling sevens (7s) or aces—a partner who has more than two sevens (7s) or two aces should discard all but two of them. Everyone should try to keep count of the number of sevens (7s) and aces in the discard pile. Remember one should always

discuss this strategy before beginning the game. Try never to discard a seven (7) unless you have at least two others in your hand. When you discard a seven (7), you are telling everyone that you have at least two more in your hand, the purpose being that if the other team starts a seven (7) canasta, they cannot complete it, because you have two sevens (7s) in your hand. Since there are only eight in the two combined decks, they cannot get more than six as long as you never discard the other two from your hand. This will lead them to being penalized 1,500 points (if three or more sevens (7s) or aces are in their hand) or 2,500 points if this column is on the table and has not been completed by the end of the round.

14. In addition, when, early in the game, you have more than three sevens (7s) in your hand, signal to your opponent by throwing out a seven (7) onto the pack. If your partner has three or more sevens (7s) in his or her hand, he or she should throw his or her sevens (7s) onto the pack at every opportunity; therefore, whichever team picks the pack will have to put down all the sevens (7s) on the table when they empty the pack. If it is your team that picks this pack, you will automatically have a head start on the completion of the sevens (7s). If there are three or more sevens (7s) in the pack, your opponents will not want to pick this pack, as they will be penalized for not completing the seven (7) canasta.

15. The preceding strategy for signaling sevens (7s) can also be used for aces.

16. Signaling wild cards—in the first round of play, a player can signal to his or her partner that he or she has four or more wild cards by discarding a high-point card (i.e., a 10- or 20-point card), and then if the partner has two or three wild cards in hand, he or she should also respond by discarding a high-point card. If your partner does not have two or three wild cards in hand, he or she should then discard a 5-point card at the next turn.

17. Near the end of a round, you might not want to pick the pack because there are too many aces or sevens (7s) in the pack. You might get caught with them, as there might not be enough turns to get rid of them and that will cost you 2,500 points for each incomplete column.

18. Toward the end of a round, you might want to throw a seven (7) (from a pair), in lieu of throwing a hot card. Keep one; throw one. Try not to throw a single seven (7) unless you have to. The same applies to aces if not shown on the table in a column.

19. If your partner picks the pack and melds three or four eights (8s), for example, and you have in your hand a pair of eights (8s), do not rush to put these two eights (8s) down on the table so that you have a pair of eights (8s) in your hand, enabling you to pick the pack should your opponent throw you an eight (8) at any time. However, if you and your partner have a lot of threes (3s) and you have no canastas as yet, then on your turn, place these two eights (8s) down just in case your partner is holding the two other matching cards to complete this canasta. Another component to this strategy is being aware of the number of cards left in the stockpile.

20. If opponents need 180 points to open (or even 155 or 125) and your team has opened with a meld and column of aces and wild cards (mixed-ace canasta), try to complete the ace canasta fast so that opponents cannot use aces to open.

21. With columns in the fifth and sixth position you and your partner should try to close 10-point canastas first (8, 9, 10, jack, queen, king) so opponents cannot use the 10-point cards in their opening or other melds or columns.

22. You might not want to put down the fifth card toward a canasta immediately, because you will be giving your opponents a safe card to throw. However, if you put down the fifth card, your partner can put down wild cards or natural cards to close the canasta but will not be able to pick the pack. This is where decision-making plays a very important role in the game.

23. If you have five of a card in your hand (possibly after picking up the pack and combining it with your hand), instead of putting all of them down, you might want to put only three down and keep two in your hand, so your opponent can throw you the card to pick the pack.

24. Begin as many columns as possible, since each one is a start toward a canasta. However, putting down all your columns and most of your cards depletes the hand and leaves you in a poor position. You are unable to pick the pack, and you cannot do much to help your partner. Try to keep some pairs in your hand so you will be able to pick the pack (contrary to the game of rummy).

25. Since five natural cards must be in each canasta, first try putting as many natural cards down as you can. Then put your wild cards down to complete the canasta. You will have a better chance to make a canasta. (With only three- or four-natural cards down on the table or two natural cards with a wild card, you are not sure the canasta will be completed.) This also prevents your opponents from creating or making this canasta.

26. If your opponents have completed two canastas (or are close to closing two canastas) and you and your partner have already melded and are saving more than two aces for an opening meld or column (A, A, A, meld or column), you should throw an ace and break up your hand so you don't get stuck with more than two aces. (You will be minus 1,500 points if left with three or more aces in your hand.)

27. If you are going for a wild card canasta and have five or six wild cards on the table, instead of picking the pack when it is your turn (especially late in the game), you should consider drawing a card from the stockpile, hoping it is a wild card. Remember if you do not make the wild card canasta, you lose 2,500 points. However, if it is a very large pack, you might want to pick the pack, hoping to make a lot of canastas, which will cut your losses from the incomplete wild card canasta. Remember there are twelve wild cards in all (eight deuces [2s] and four jokers).

You should always count how many are on the table and how many have been used to make completed canastas. Then you know if it is possible for you to make your wild-card canasta.

28. After you pick the pack and lay down your cards, try to wait one turn before closing canastas with wild cards. Rationale—your partner may have the natural card(s) in his or her hand, and the wild cards would be wasted.

29. Reasons for going out quickly include the following:

☐ The other team is not open yet, and you want them to be minus everything.

☐ The other team is ready to go out.

☐ You want to protect your threes (3s) (get the bonus points).

☐ The other team started a special canasta (aces, sevens [7s], wild cards), and you don't want them to complete it.

☐ You get 100 points for going out.

# 9
# ♥
## CHAPTER

# Special Hands and Canastas

All these special hands consist of fourteen cards, and for all these special hands, the game stops and your opponents count their points as if the game were finished regularly.

## SEVENS

A canasta of sevens must always be clean—that is, it may never have a wild card. If completed, it is worth 2,500 points. If not completed, it is worth minus 2,500 points. If you have three or more sevens (7s) in your hand, your score is minus 1,500 points.

## ACES

A canasta of aces may be made with (only upon opening) or without wild cards. If started without wild cards, it must then be completed without wild cards. If completed, it is worth 2,500 points. If not completed, it is worth minus 2,500 points.

The only time an ace canasta may have wild cards is when it is used in the opening or initial meld. Then it is treated as any dirty or mixed canasta, and if completed, it is worth 300 points. There is no penalty if it is not completed.

## JOKERS

A canasta consists of seven (7) wild cards with the following values. Any combination of jokers and deuces (2s) is worth 2,500 points. If you complete a wild card canasta with all deuces (2s), it is worth 3,000 points. Once a wild card canasta is started, you cannot use a wild card on any other started canasta until this wild card canasta is completed. If a wild card canasta is not completed, it is worth a score of minus 2,500 points. Conversely, one cannot start a wild card canasta during a round, providing there are wild cards already on the melds or columns.

## PAIRS

A canasta that consists of seven pairs (fourteen cards). All pairs must be of different rank (number value). Threes cannot be used in a pairs hand. Once a team has melded, the partner cannot go for a pair hand. If you have a pair of deuces (2s), then you must

have a pair of sevens and a pair of aces (or any
combination of these three cards—for example, if
you have a pair of sevens [7s], then you must also have
a pair of aces and a pair of like wild cards). You
cannot pair a deuce with a joker. If you have a pair of
jokers, you must have a pair of sevens and a pair of
aces. If you have a pair of wild cards (either two big
jokers or two deuces), then you must have a pair of
sevens (7s) and a pair of aces. When the pairs hand
is melded, the game stops. This is worth 3,500 points.
The partner's hand does not count (even if the partner
has three aces or sevens (7s) in hand), and this hand
is not penalized. Threes (3s) are now ignored. The
other team scores as if the game ended normally.

Note—should you have aces or sevens (7s) in your hand, you have
the option of discarding these before the completion of your special
pairs hand, thus you will not need a pair of sevens plus a pair of aces
plus a pair of wild cards.

## GARBAGE HAND

You must have one of everything, including a big
joker and a three. The fourteen cards must be ace, 2,
3, 4, 5, 6, 7, 8, 9, 10, jack, queen, king, and big joker.
They may be of different suits (i.e., not all hearts,
diamonds, spades, or clubs). The game stops, and this
is worth 3,500 points. Your partner's hand does not
count. No threes are counted either. The other team

scores normally. Once a team is melded, you cannot go for a garbage
hand. If the other team goes out (ends the game) before you meld or
open with a garbage hand, then the threes in your hand count against
you as if they were on the table.

## SPLASH (OR AUTOMATIC MELD)

A splash is a clean, pure, or natural canasta in your hand (i.e., all the same numbers, for example, 9, 9, 9, 9, 9, 9, 9) to open. This can be melded on the table without having the necessary count to open. If you are lucky enough to open with this, it is automatically worth 3,500 points. This eliminates the need for the required opening minimum. This splash hand may also include pure melds or canastas of sevens (7s), aces, or deuces (2s). The game stops.

You may open with a seven-card canasta and avoid the minimum melds or canastas, but you must have the seven cards in your hand. You cannot pick a discarded card to make the seventh one; it must come from the stockpile (and not the pack). The game stops.

## A TABLE RULE

Some play such that if you have one seven-card canasta from your hand, it is melded on the table without needing the necessary count to open. At some tables, the game continues in the regular fashion, and you do not obtain the 3,500 points but rather 2,500 points.

However, during the game, once you and your partner have opened and you have accumulated seven identical face cards in your hand, expose them to everyone, and this will give you and your partner an additional 2,500 points. The game continues.

## 2,3,4,5,

If you have 2,3,4,5 (two of a kind, three of a kind, four of a kind, five of a kind equaling fourteen cards, for example, 4,4; 6,6,6; 8,8,8,8; and jack, jack, jack, jack, jack) the game stops. This is worth 3,500 points. Your partner's hand does not count (even if the partner has three aces or sevens (7s) in hand, and it is not penalized). The threes are ignored. Once a team has melded, you cannot go for a special hand. The other team scores as if the game had ended normally.

## 3,3,4,4

If you have 3, 3, 4, 4 (three of a kind, three of a kind, four of a kind, four of a kind, equaling fourteen cards, for example, 5, 5, 5; king, king, king; 9, 9, 9, 9; and queen, queen, queen, queen), the game stops. This is worth 3,500 points. Your partner's hand does not count (even if the partner has three aces or sevens (7s) in hand, and it is not penalized). The threes are  ignored. Once a team has melded, you cannot go for a special hand. The other team scores as if the game had ended normally.

## 3,3,3,3 PLUS TWO IDENTICAL WILD CARDS

If you have 3, 3, 3, 3 plus two identical wild cards (three of a kind, three of a kind, three of a kind, three of a kind plus two identical wild cards equaling fourteen cards, for example, 4, 4, 4; 6, 6, 6; king, king, king; and 9, 9, 9 plus two identical wild cards), the game stops. This is worth 3,500 points. Your partner's hand does not count (even if the partner  has three aces or three sevens, and it is not penalized). The threes are ignored. Once a team has melded, you cannot go for a special hand. The other team scores as if the game had ended normally.

## 4,4,4, PLUS TWO IDENTICAL WILD CARDS

If you have 4, 4, 4 plus two identical wild cards (four of a kind, four of a kind, four of a kind plus two identical wild cards equaling fourteen cards, for example, 4, 4, 4, 4; 6, 6, 6, 6; king, king, king, king plus two identical wild cards), the game stops. This is worth 3,500 points. Your partner's hand does not count (even if the partner has three aces or three sevens, and it is not penalized). The threes are ignored. Once a team has melded, you cannot go for a special hand. The other team scores as if the game ended normally.

## 3,3,3,3 PLUS ONE IDENTICAL PAIR

If you have four sets of three of a kind plus one identical pair, fourteen cards (three of a kind, three of a kind, three of a kind, three of a kind plus two identical face cards equaling fourteen cards, for example, 4, 4, 4; 6, 6, 6; 8, 8, 8; and queen, queen, queen plus 9, 9), the game stops. The pair cannot be identical to the existing sets. This is worth 3,500

points. Your partner's hand does not count (even if the partner has three aces or three sevens, and it is not penalized). The threes are ignored. Once a team has melded, you cannot go for a special hand. The other team scores as if the game ended normally.

## 4,4,4 PLUS ONE IDENTICAL PAIR

If you have three sets of four of a kind plus one identical pair, fourteen cards (four of a kind, four of a kind, four of a kind plus two identical face cards equaling fourteen cards, for example, 4, 4, 4, 4; 5, 5, 5, 5; and 10, 10, 10, 10 plus 8, 8), the game stops. The pair cannot be identical to the existing sets. This is worth 3,500 points. Your partner's hand does not

count (even if your partner has three aces or three sevens, and it is not penalized). The threes are ignored. Once a team has melded, you cannot go for a special hand. The other team scores as if the game had ended normally.

## TWO CANASTAS IN HAND

Two canastas in hand—if you have two dirty canastas (with wild cards) in your hand, fourteen cards (five or six of a kind with one or two wild cards to complete one canasta and another five or six of a kind with one or two wild cards to complete the second canasta), the game stops. This hand is worth 3,500 points. This also includes the possibility of having one clean canasta as well as a dirty canasta. This also equals 3,500 points, and the game stops, as long as you have two canastas in your hand (fourteen cards). Your partner's hand does not count (even if your partner has three aces or sevens in hand, and it is not penalized). Threes are ignored. Once the team is melded, you cannot go for a special hand. The other team scores as if the game had ended normally.

## QUICK SUMMARY

1. Five of a kind of two different numbers plus four jokers or wild cards equal fourteen cards (same as two canastas in hand, as above)
2. Four sets of three of a kind plus two identical jokers or wild cards equal fourteen cards
3. Four sets of three of a kind plus one identical pair equal fourteen cards
4. Three sets of four of a kind plus two identical jokers or wild cards equal fourteen cards

All these special hands, which include a total of fourteen cards, are worth 3,500 points each.

# CHAPTER

# Playing Canasta with Two Players

What if you schedule a game with three of your friends and then suddenly two of them have an unexpected commitment to take care of? Do you cancel the afternoon or evening, or do the two remaining people get together to play a slightly different form of the already-learned game?

Canasta with two players is basically the same game with a few changes. You are actually playing the game without a partner—you *are* your partner!

Here are the rules for playing with two players:

1. Fifteen cards are dealt to each player (rather than the original thirteen).

2. The cutter uses the bottom cards of the cut deck to make piles (the talons) as follows: three piles of four cards and one pile of

three cards (thus totalling 15 cards). The first and third pile of four cards are combined and placed under the stockpile, and the middle pile of four is placed around the tray as is the last pile of three cards, thus making two talons—one of four cards and one of three cards to be picked up during the game when each player opens.

3. If a three (3) is in one of these two piles (talons), you do not replace it with another card upon your turn. This becomes a table rule.

4. When picking from the stockpile, you draw the top two cards at every turn, but only discard one card as usual. Therefore, during the game, you are constantly accumulating more cards in your hand.

5. No dream hands come into play during the game.

6. The game ends when one of the players reaches 8,500 points.

7. As usual, you need two canastas to go out.

## CHAPTER

# Playing Canasta with Three Players

What if you schedule a game with three of your friends and then suddenly one of them has an unexpected commitment to take care of? Do you cancel the afternoon or evening, or do the three remaining people get together to play a slightly different form of the already-learned game?

Canasta with three players is basically the same game with a few changes. You are actually playing the game without a partner. You are your partner!

Here are the rules for playing with three players:

1. One person cuts the shuffled deck.
2. The top section of the deck is used for the talon distribution (using eighteen cards). The remaining pack is used to deal the three fifteen-card hands (total of forty-five cards).

Tip—remember T (top), T (talon), B (bottom), D (deal) = (T–T; B–D).

3. The person to the left of the cutter deals fifteen cards to each of the three players. These cards are dealt clockwise.

4. While the dealer is dealing, the cutter makes five piles from the bottom of the deck (i.e., one pile of five cards, two piles of four cards, one pile of three cards, and one pile of two cards). This totals eighteen cards (T–T; B–D).

5. The cutter then collects the first pile of five cards and the second pile of four and combines them and then places them across the tray under the stockpile of unexposed cards, thus showing that the end of the game is near when playing. There will be nine cards in this pile, thus indicating approximately three more turns each for each of the players.

6. The four-card, three-card, and two-card piles are placed on the sides of the tray facedown and considered your talons. These piles are picked up during the game by each player after melding. If a three (3) is in one of these two piles, you do not replace it with another card upon your turn. This becomes a table rule.

7. The game (play) always goes clockwise (i.e., the first person to play is left of the dealer).

8. The object is to get as many points as possible.

9. To win the game, one must reach 8,500 points.

10. Place like cards together. Begin the game. Place threes (3s) facedown on the table, and when it is your turn, face them up as you replace those cards. (Threes (3s) are never used for melding.) The player to the left of the dealer picks a top card from the pile and discards one from their hand. Each player, in turn, continues in this manner until one of the partners has enough points to open, placing the melds or columns open in front of him or her.

11. Canastas can have up to two wild cards.

12. The first person to open gets the four-card pile. The second person to open receives the three-card pile, and the last person to open receives the remaining two-card pile.

13. Pick up the talon immediately after melding, or you will lose it. You snooze, you lose!

14. If no one opens, then the talons remain untouched.

15. To meld (to put down on the table), you must have at least three like cards (a triple) or more and two like cards with a wild card, and what you put down must add up to the 125/155/180 points or more to start.

16. To go out, you must have at least two canastas. It makes no difference if they are natural or mixed, and you must end with a strange or foreign card.

17. If you have only one canasta at the end of the game, then your threes (3s) are not counted for any points; they become neutral.

18. If you have no canastas at the end of the game, then all your points are counted as minus (including the threes [3s]).

19. If you pick up the pack to open or meld, you must have three face cards of that top card on the pack.

20. If you pick up the pack during the game, once you have opened, you must have two face cards of that top card on the pack. Remember if you are picking the pack to open, you must have three face cards of that top card on the pack.

21. If you pick up the pack, you must put down your cards from your hand. You cannot combine these cards with the cards from the pack.

22. During the play, a natural canasta (all face value cards with no wild cards) in your hand (and not picked from the discarded pile) is a special hand and does not end the game. This is one of the special hands, which is now worth 2,500 points, as the game does not stop.

23. The only special hand possible while playing three players are pairs (i.e., 8 pairs = 16 cards), two canastas in hand, and, instead of the 3, 3, 4, 4 hand, a 4, 4, 4, 4 hand. Each of these are worth 3,500 points, and the game stops. Your partner is not penalized

for any sevens (7s) or aces in his or her hand, and your threes (3s) are not counted as well. Your opponents count their points as if the game ended regularly.

24. You must empty the pack when you pick it up—that is, any card that matches what is already down (even one card) or anything that you have three or more of in the pack (even sevens [7s] and aces) must be put down.

25. Once started, you must finish the wild card canasta before adding any other wild cards to other incomplete canastas.

26. Wild cards can never be used with sevens (7s).

27. A wild card can be used on opening or melding when combined with aces. However, the value of this completed canasta is only 300 points. If not completed, you are not penalized. This is the only time you can use wild cards with aces.

28. However, when opening or starting a clean ace meld (your option) during the hand (i.e., without wild cards), if you do not complete it, you are penalized 2,500 points. Wild cards can never be placed on this meld or column during the round.

29. During the game, you must put two cards down at a time from your hand, but if it is to finish a canasta (sixth position), you can put one card down only. This rule must be discussed prior to starting your game.

30. To go out or finish the hand, you must have at least two canastas, and you need a strange card to discard. You earn an extra 100 points for going out.

31. When the stockpile is completed, normally the game ends. If, however, the person next in rotation has two or more face cards matching the last card thrown, he or she may pick the pack, if desired. They then put down all relevant cards from the pack and discard their last strange or foreign card, thus ending the game.

32. The game ends when one team reaches 8,500 points.

# CHAPTER

# Playing Canasta with Six Players

What if you schedule a game with three of your friends and then suddenly two of them have another friend who wants to join your game?

Canasta with six players is basically the same game with some changes.

Here are the rules for playing with six players:

1. Three decks of 52 cards are used along with 6 jokers and 12 deuces (2s), equaling 162 cards in total.
2. There are options built into this game with multiple players. There can be three teams of two players with the partners sitting opposite (ideally at a round table), or there can be two teams of three players with each player sitting between their opponents and one player sitting out at the next play.
3. Thirteen cards are dealt to each player.
4. The cutter uses the bottom 15 cards of the cut deck to make four piles, consisting of three piles of four cards and one pile

of three cards. As in our rules for how to play with four people, there are two talons placed around the tray—one pile consisting of four cards and one pile consisting of three cards. The other two piles of four cards are combined and placed at the bottom of the stockpile.

5. The special hands come into play during the game and are counted the same way as if you were playing with four players.

6. Therefore, the game is identical to that when playing with four people.

7. The game ends when one of the players reaches 8,500 points.

8. As usual, you need two canastas to go out.

## CHAPTER 13

# Samba Canasta Rules

## (PLAYED WITH FOUR PEOPLE AND SIX DECKS OF CARDS)

**Samba :** A samba is a run of seven consecutive cards, for example, eight, nine, ten, jack, queen, king, ace. A samba must be of one suit. A samba must be started from the cards in your hand and not from picking the top card from the pack. A wild card can never be used in the samba. *Table Rule:* The samba can never be started, using a seven (7), until your canasta of sevens have been completed.

**How to Play:** Each player is dealt two packs of fifteen cards each. The play begins when the player to the left of the dealer cuts the cards. The dealer deals four piles of fifteen cards. A pile is given to each player. This is called the **hand**. At the same time the cutter deals four piles of fifteen cards. A pile is given to each player. This is called the **foot**.

You start your turn by always picking up two cards at a time. You are allowed to place as little as one card down at a time, or as many as all of the cards in your hand. If you put down all of your cards from your hand, and you do not have a discard to throw to end your turn, you must pick up all of the cards from the foot and choose one card from those fifteen cards. Table Rule—-You may put down as many cards from the foot as you desire, should you use all of the cards from your hand. To end your turn, you must throw out a card onto the pack. However, during your turn, if you put down all of your cards from your hand and still have a discard, you must put down that card from your hand to end your turn. You then can pick up the cards from the foot. However, you cannot play from these cards until your next turn.

The dealer begins the play. Every player takes two cards from the stockpile to start their turn, and throws one card onto the pack to end their turn. In order to open, you must have the required points per round (see below). The object of the game is to complete these six requirements:

1.  You and your partner must both be playing from the cards from the foot;
2.  You and your partner must complete a minimum of at least **five red canastas** (canastas without any wild cards). Five completed red canastas is called a Book;
3.  You and your partner must complete a minimum of at least **one black canasta** (a canasta with one or two wild cards);
4.  You and your partner must complete a minimum of at least **one wild card canasta** (a canasta consisting of all twos or a canasta consisting of a mixture of twos and big jokers);
5.  You and your partner must complete a minimum of at least **one canasta of sevens**. This canasta can never contain wild cards; and
6.  You and your partner must complete a minimum of at least **one samba**. This canasta must be of one suit and can never contain wild cards;

To open, you need :    1st round - 50 points
2nd round - 90 points
3rd round - 120 points
4th round - 150 points

If you do not meet your round requirements and there are no cards left in the stockpile, you turn over the pack and continue the play. This is done only once during a round.

A canasta of aces can never contain wild cards. This canasta is considered to be part of the five red completed canastas needed to end the game. *Table Rule :* This canasta may be started with wild cards at any time during the game.

A canasta of sevens can never contain wild cards. *Table Rule:* This canasta must be completed before you and your partner can start a samba canasta that contains a seven in its run. Or, you may start a samba before finishing a canasta of sevens, but this samba never can contain a seven in its run until your canasta of sevens have been completed.

You may throw black threes onto the pack. This can never be picked up by any player. These are considered safe or frozen cards.

You may throw a wild card onto the pack only if you have nothing else to discard. However, no one can pick up this wild card to start a canasta.

You and your partner do not have to put any cards down during your turn. You and your partner may put down as many cards as you desire. You are allowed to place one card down at a time as desired.

To open, you must have three face cards of the top card in order to pick the pack. Once you have opened and to be able to pick the pack you must have either two of a kind of that same top card on the pack, or one of a kind and a wild card.

Whenever you pick the pack, you only take the top eight cards.

Once you and your partner have accomplished the six requirements of the game, you may go out by disposing all of the cards in your hand. You do not need a final card to throw onto the pack. This gives this team and additional 500 points.

Wild cards can never be included in canastas of aces, sevens, or sambas.

Scoring :  Red three            -   100 points
           Red canasta          -   500 points
           Black canasta        -   300 points
           Wildcard canasta     -   2,000 points
           Canasta of sevens    -   2,000 points
           Samba canasta        -   1,000 points
           Team going out       -   500 points
           To win the game      -   100,000 points (or highest score)

Total scoring of each hand is calculated the same as for can(am) asta™. The base points are all your canasta requirements. Meld points is the total of all of your cards in both your completed and incomplete canastas. There are no penalties for non-completion of any canasta.

Enjoy!

## SCORE SHEET FOR SAMBA:

| Accomplishments | Us | They | Accomplishments | Us | They |
|---|---|---|---|---|---|
| Red Threes (100 points) | | | Red Threes (100 points) | | |
| Red Canastas (500 points) | | | Red Canastas (500 points) | | |
| Black Canastas (300 points) | | | Black Canastas (300 points) | | |
| Wild Card Canastas (2,000 points) | | | Wild Card Canastas (2,000 points) | | |
| Seven Canasta (2,000 points) | | | Seven Canasta (2,000 points) | | |
| Samba Canasta (1,000 points) | | | Samba Canasta (1,000 points) | | |
| Going Out (500 points) | | | Going Out (500 points) | | |
| Meld Score (card points) | | | Meld Score (card points) | | |
| Subtotal | | | Subtotal | | |
| **TOTAL** | | | **TOTAL** | | |
| Red Threes (100 points) | | | Red Threes (100 points) | | |
| Red Canastas (500 points) | | | Red Canastas (500 points) | | |
| Black Canastas (300 points) | | | Black Canastas (300 points) | | |
| Wild Card Canastas (2,000 points) | | | Wild Card Canastas (2,000 points) | | |
| Seven Canasta (2,000 points) | | | Seven Canasta (2,000 points) | | |
| Samba Canasta (1,000 points) | | | Samba Canasta (1,000 points) | | |
| Going Out (500 points) | | | Going Out (500 points) | | |
| Meld Score (card points) | | | Meld Score (card points) | | |
| Subtotal | | | Subtotal | | |
| **TOTAL** | | | **TOTAL** | | |

# CHAPTER

## Variations / Table Rules

Before starting the game, players should always agree in advance to their table rules and variations. All players should agree.

### COMPLETED GAME

Some play such that the game is over when one of the partners reaches 10,000 points.

### SIGNALING SEVENS (7S) OR ACES OR WILD CARDS

Some play such that when you discard a seven (7) or an ace during the play, you are signaling to your partner that you have an additional two more sevens (7s) or aces in your hand. Others play such that this is never a signal. Remember you should always discuss this strategy before beginning the game. Try never to discard a seven (7) unless you have at least two others in your hand. Remember signaling is a very important component of a challenging and exciting game.

## STRANGE CARD

For some players, a strange card can be a card identical to an incomplete canasta (e.g., if you have a meld or column of fives (5, 5, 5, 5), you may throw a five out as your last card because your column of fives is not considered a completed canasta! Also, some play so that a strange card can be a wild card.

## TO PICK THE PACK UPON OPENING

Some play according to the rule that you do not require three identical face cards to pick the pack upon opening; you need only two identical cards. However, the top card on the pack does not count for your total required points for opening or any other partial or completed canastas obtained from picking the pack. Also, some play so that you still require the three identical face cards to pick the pack upon opening, and again, the top card on the pack does not count for your total required points for opening.

At some tables, you may combine your hand with the pack that you just picked and may, therefore, discard all variations pertinent to your opening melds or columns. Some play so that if you pick the pack to open, you do not get the bonus pack (the talon). Your opponents, after opening, get the three-card talon, and the four-card talon remains unused during that round of play.

## UPON OPENING

Some play such that you do not need the required meld or column of three natural cards for your initial meld; therefore, any collection of melds or columns worth enough points is sufficient.

# HOLDING BACK THREES (3S)

To avoid the larger negative score for threes on the table, if your team has not opened, at some tables, you are allowed to hold the threes in your hand and not put them on the table. These threes would give you a minus score of 5 each, rather than the usual minus 100, 300, 500, or 1,000 should you not be lucky enough to open or to make one completed canasta.

# WHEN THE LAST CARD OF THE STOCKPILE IS A THREE (3)

Some play so that the game ends immediately and the three (3) counts as 5 points against the team that drew this card; therefore, it is not counted in the other threes (3s) obtained during the game. Or the player has the option to meld the three (3). Since no replacement card can be drawn, the play ends immediately. Or the player must meld it even if the team has not completed any canastas, therefore incurring a penalty of 100 or more points for the three (3). The play subsequently ends since there is no replacement card available. Or the three (3) can be discarded as the strange card if the player is able to go out and end the game.

Please remember that these rules are all options, and remember to discuss them before playing the game.

# WHEN A THREE (3) IS IN ONE OF THE LAST EIGHT CARDS OF THE STOCK

At some tables, the three is never replaced by another card from the stockpile. You may include this three in your basic point count, but you never replace it with another card.

# TAKING THE PACK

Some play such that the player making the initial meld for their team is not allowed to take the pack even if he or she had the additional triple with which to take the card. The pack can only be taken if you or your partner have already made its initial meld or opening.

## BOTTOM OF PACK TALON

At some tables, before placing the eight remaining cards of the pack in the opposite direction of the pack, they place a ninth card in a different direction, thus signaling the remaining eight cards where you cannot replace a three (3) should you receive one in the last eight cards.

## RULE OF FIVE

Some play such that when you have an initial clean meld or column of three or four cards (e.g., 4, 4, 4 or 4, 4, 4, 4), you cannot place a wild card onto this meld or column until there are five face cards in this particular meld or column.

## SIZE OF YOUR CANASTAS

At some tables, if you have all eight face cards of the particular canasta, you can put them all down in your completed canasta. That means if you have a completed canasta (king, king, king, king, king, two wild cards), you may put down the remaining three kings, if you have them at the time of completion of this canasta.

## PICKING THE PACK—ANYTIME DURING THE GAME

Some play such that you can combine the pack with your hand before placing all the required cards from the pack onto the started columns and placing all three or more cards to start a column.

# WHEN PLAYING THE SPECIAL HAND OF PAIRS

At some tables, you do not necessarily need seven different pairs to complete this hand. You may have, for example, five different pairs and four identical face cards, thus equaling two identical pairs and the five different pairs.

# TO GO OUT

Some play such that you are allowed to place only one card on a column that is in a third, fourth, or fifth position and then throw a strange card, enabling you to go out.

At some tables, a team cannot ever go out if they have an incomplete canasta of sevens, pure aces, or wild cards. If your team starts a sevens meld or column, a pure ace meld or column, or a wild card meld or column, you must complete the canasta before you can go out.

# SPLASH HAND

At some tables, if you have seven identical face cards, the game stops, and this is worth 3,500 points.

For some, when you get seven (7) identical face cards, you place them down on the table and you do not require the total amount of points needed to open. The game continues, and this does not give you any additional points for having these cards.

Some play such that you need two sets of seven (7) identical face cards (fourteen cards) for the game to stop and for this to be worth 3,500 points. However, during the game, once you and your partner have opened and you have accumulated seven identical face cards in your hand, you expose them to everyone, and this will give you and your partner an additional 2,500 points, and the game continues.

## HAND AND FOOT

Some play such that an extra hand is dealt to each player, consisting of three to five cards (another table rule). These extra cards would be picked up and played when you have not completed two canastas and have used up all the cards in your hand.

# 15

## CHAPTER

# FAQ

**1. Can you think of a situation where it is a poor idea to pick the pack?**

When you are left holding aces, sevens (7s), or both and do not make enough points to cover that loss because there are not enough turns left to discard the excess sevens (7s) or aces or the other team, which was trying to go out, does so. This is one reason why it is so very important to know how many sevens (7s) and aces are in that discarded pack.

**2. Should you ever pick the pack if you know you definitely will get caught with aces or sevens (7s)?**

Yes, if you will make enough points to offset the negative points. For example, your team has made no canastas, you have accumulated 800 points or more in threes (3s), and there are a lot of cards in the discarded pack. With no canastas, the threes (3s) are negative. If you have completed two canastas or more, the threes (3s) are full value, which will not offset the 2,500 points for getting penalized with sevens (7s) or aces but will give you more points to offset your loss.

3.  *Is there ever a time when you want your opponent to pick the pack, when you throw a hot card (seven (7) or ace)?*

Yes, if you believe your team can go out quickly and catch them with sevens (7s) or aces.

4.  *Should I ever discard a third card of a set (e.g., you have three eights [8s] and discard one of them)?*

Yes, your team is open, and it is early in the hand. This is called "bait"—you want your opponent, particularly the one to your right (i.e., the person who throws you their discarded card), to think you do not have this card. They throw it, and you pick the pack.

5.  *If I have five of a kind in my hand and my team is open, should I lay out all five cards?*

No, early in the game, you may want to lay down three and hold two back (could mean you open two sixes [6s] with a wild card and keep two sixes [6s] in your hand). Maybe your opponent will think that it is a safe card to discard since you were the one to open that threesome. They throw it, and you pick the pack. If your team is trying to get out quickly, however, lay out all five. Late in the hand, lay out all five, as you want to give your team every chance to make another canasta before the hand ends.

6.  *During the round, can you ever start a wild card canasta if there is a wild card already on the table in one of your melds or columns?*

No, because you can never have wild cards in any other meld or column until that wild card canasta is completed. You must complete those melds or columns (canastas) before starting a wild card canasta.

## 7. *Can you ever have two identical canastas on the same round?*

No, because once a canasta is made with fives (e.g., 5-5-5-5-5-5-5 or 5-5-5-5-5-2 wild cards), you have one to three fives left in the deck. If you have two or three fives left, at some tables, you can start another canasta with these fives accompanied with a wild card. However, our game does not permit this. This could be included in your table rules, if so warranted.

## 8. *If you have a full canasta in your hand, is the game stopped?*

Generally, no, game is only stopped if you have two full clean or dirty canastas in your hand, totalling fourteen cards. According to some players' rules, the game is stopped. This comes down to deciding your table rules before playing.

## 9. *How do you know if your opponents are planning to go out quickly?*

- ☐ if your opponents have completed two canastas
- ☐ if your opponents are not picking the pack
- ☐ if your opponents have three or fewer cards in their hands

CHAPTER

# Playing Canasta for Money

(Optional but Lots of Fun!)

1. Everyone brings five dollars to play—preferably five one-dollar bills or coins.

2. At the end of each round, the score is tallied, and each of these important completions and noncompletions is recognized:

   - The team that scores the highest points of that round receives $1.00 from each of their opponents.

   - The team that cuts the exact amount of cards for the dealer (e.g., 13 x 4 = 52 cards) receives $1.00 from each of their opponents.

   - The team that accomplishes the completion a canasta of special hands, any of these or all of these, receives $1.00 from each of their opponents. Each accomplishment is recognized.

- The team that does not complete a canasta of sevens (7s), mixed wild cards, all deuces (2s), or pure aces gives to each of their opponents $1.00. Each incompletion is recognized.
- The team that is caught holding three or more sevens (7s) or aces at the end of the round gives $1.00 to each of their opponents. For example, if caught with more than three sevens (7s) and three aces, they give each of their opponents 2 x $1.00 = $2.00.
- The team that opens with the incorrect amount of points will have to give $1.00 to each of their opponents.
- The team that is not able to open during the whole game gives their opponents $1.00 each.
- The team that wins at the end of the game receives $1.00 from each of their opponents.
- The team that goes out receives $1.00 from each of their opponents.
- The team that picks up all the threes (3s) (four reds and four blacks) receives $1.00 from each opponent.

Note

If at any time during the game one team loses the total $5.00, then the game continues on the house. However, their opponents do have to pay them if it is warranted, and the payment of $1.00 for each accomplishment or nonaccomplishment resumes.

*Hinda Packard and Nancy Kaplan*

## CAN(AM)ASTA™ SCORE SHEET

|  | We | They |  | We | They |
|---|---|---|---|---|---|
| Base |  |  | Base |  |  |
| Count |  |  | Count |  |  |
| **Total** |  |  | **Total** |  |  |
| Base |  |  | Base |  |  |
| Count |  |  | Count |  |  |
| **Total** |  |  | **Total** |  |  |
| Base |  |  | Base |  |  |
| Count |  |  | Count |  |  |
| **Total** |  |  | **Total** |  |  |
| Base |  |  | Base |  |  |
| Count |  |  | Count |  |  |
| **Total** |  |  | **Total** |  |  |
| Base |  |  | Base |  |  |
| Count |  |  | Count |  |  |
| **Total** |  |  | **Total** |  |  |
| Base |  |  | Base |  |  |
| Count |  |  | Count |  |  |
| **Total** |  |  | **Total** |  |  |
| Base |  |  | Base |  |  |
| Count |  |  | Count |  |  |
| **Total** |  |  | **Total** |  |  |
| Base |  |  | Base |  |  |
| Count |  |  | Count |  |  |
| **Total** |  |  | **Total** |  |  |

| Calculation Pad |  |  |  |
|---|---|---|---|
|  |  |  |  |
|  |  |  |  |

# Conclusion

We have come to the end of this handbook, and we realize that in reality there really is never an ending to the wonderful game of canasta. What we mean by that is that there will always be a new rule that you might be faced with—as knowledge is power. The more you learn, the more you learn; the more you know, the more you know. To embrace this, we suggest that whenever you play canasta with a new person, always start your game by asking, "What are your table rules?"

Oprah Winfrey is a great role model. Her perseverance, her honesty, and her integrity are qualities that we admire. So if I may borrow from her, this is "what I know for sure":

☐ The game of canasta(am)asta™ will give you many hours of enjoyment, joy, and peace.
☐ The game of canasta(am)asta™ will bring new and old friends into your life.
☐ The game of canasta(am)asta™ may just well be the elixir to a happier life in general.

We wish you all the very best and many hours of enjoyment with this exciting game.

Hinda Packard with Nancy Kaplan

Printed in the United States
By Bookmasters